ICONS

History Makers

Henry Ford

by Pamela McDowell

AV² provides enriched content that supplements and complements this book. Weigl's AV² books strive to create inspired learning and engage young minds in a total learning experience.

Your AV² Media Enhanced books come alive with...

Audio
Listen to sections of the book read aloud.

Key Words
Study vocabulary, and complete a matching word activity.

Video
Watch informative video clips.

Quizzes
Test your knowledge.

Embedded Weblinks
Gain additional information for research.

Slide Show
View images and captions, and prepare a presentation.

Try This!
Complete activities and hands-on experiments.

... and much, much more!

Go to **www.av2books.com,** and enter this book's unique code.

BOOK CODE

V934427

AV² by Weigl brings you media enhanced books that support active learning.

Published by AV² by Weigl
350 5th Avenue, 59th Floor
New York, NY 10118

www.av2books.com   www.weigl.com

Library of Congress Cataloging-in-Publication Data

McDowell, Pamela.
  Henry Ford / Pamela McDowell.
    page cm. -- (Icons)
  Audience: Grade 4 to 6.
  Includes index.
  ISBN 978-1-62127-306-6 (hardcover : alk. paper) -- ISBN 978-1-62127-312-7 (softcover : alk. paper)
  1. Ford, Henry, 1863-1947--Juvenile literature. 2. Industrialists--United States--Biography--Juvenile literature. 3. Automobile engineers--United States--Biography--Juvenile literature. 4. Automobile industry and trade--United States--Juvenile literature. I. Title.
  TL140.F6M336 2014
  338.7'629222092--dc23
  [B]
                        2012041284

Printed in the United States of America in North Mankato, Minnesota
2 3 4 5 6 7 8 9 0 18 17 16 15 14

WEP300714
072014

Editor: Megan Cuthbert
Design: Tammy West

Photograph Credits
Weigl acknowledges Getty Images as the primary image supplier for this title. Every reasonable effort has been made to trace ownership and to obtain permission to reprint copyright material. The publishers would be pleased to have any errors or omissions brought to their attention so that they may be corrected in subsequent printings.

Contents

Who Was Henry Ford?

Henry Ford is known as the father of the Model T. The Model T was the world's first affordable automobile. Henry wanted to build a machine that would change the way people lived. He devoted his life to improving how cars were made. The Model T was affordable enough that most people could buy one. Once they owned cars, people no longer needed horses to travel. They could travel greater distances to get to work and go on vacations.

Henry changed the way business and **manufacturing** worked. He created a way to produce many vehicles quickly, and with lower costs. Other industries soon copied his methods. Henry also introduced many changes that helped the workers in his factories.

"I do not want the things money can buy. I want to live a life, to make the world a little better for (my) having lived in it."

Growing Up

Henry Ford was born in Michigan on July 30, 1863. His parents, William and Mary, raised their family on a farm near present-day Dearborn. Henry was the oldest of six children. He tinkered with the farm machines and fixed broken watches. His younger brothers and sisters hid their toys from Henry because he loved to take them apart to see how they worked.

Henry was traveling with his father when he saw the first road engine that was not pulled by horses. The driver was happy to stop and explain to the 12-year-old boy how the machine worked. Henry was inspired. Now he knew what he wanted to do with his life. At the age of 15, Henry constructed his first engine. It was a steam engine.

▲ **Dearborn, Michigan is home to the Henry Ford Museum. The first artifacts displayed in the museum were from Henry's personal collection.**

Get to Know
Michigan

CANADA

N

LAKE HURON

LAKE ONTARIO

WISCONSIN

MICHIGAN

LAKE MICHIGAN

LAKE ERIE

The state capital of Michigan is Lansing. Detroit is the state's most populated city, with more than 700,000 people.

Car manufacturers such as Ford, Chrysler, and General Motors have their headquarters in or near Detroit.

Detroit's nickname is Motown. It is a short form of 'motor town,' and a reference to the city's popular music label, Motown Records.

Michigan is made up of two peninsulas connected by the Mackinac Bridge. A peninsula is a piece of land bordered by water on three sides.

STATE SYMBOLS

TREE
Eastern White Pine

BIRD
American Robin

FLOWER
Apple Blossom

Practice Makes Perfect

When he was 16, Henry left the family farm for Detroit. He worked for several different machine shops before getting a job at Westinghouse Engine Company. Here, Henry learned about different kinds of engines. In 1891, Henry got a job at the Edison Illuminating Company. He was promoted to chief engineer there in 1893. During his time at the company, Henry learned about electricity. He was also introduced to the company's owner and fellow inventor, Thomas Edison. With Thomas's support, Henry continued to develop his ideas for a **self-propelled** vehicle.

After his experiment with a steam engine as a child, Henry decided to build a new type of engine, using gas instead. His first gas engine combined gas and air in a single **cylinder**. Electricity provided the spark to ignite the mixture. Henry completed his 'quadricycle' in 1896. It had four bike wheels and was steered using a long metal bar. When it was finished, Henry realized he could not fit the quadricycle out of the workshop door. He had to tear down part of a wall before he took his first test drive.

◀ Henry worked at the Edison Illuminating Company for eight years. His job gave him the time and money to pursue his personal experiments with engines.

In 1899, Henry formed the Detroit Automobile Company. The new company's first vehicle was a delivery wagon. Then, Henry made a car that reached about 72 miles (115.9 km) per hour. He entered the car in a race on October 10, 1901, and won. Henry then built the '999', which was named after a famous steam train. In 1902, the 999 won a 5-mile (8-km) race. Racing helped create publicity for Henry's cars. It also gave him the chance to make improvements to his car design.

QUICK FACTS

- The Model T was nicknamed "Tin Lizzie." Lizzie was a slang word for a servant who was dependable.

- The top speed of Ford's quadricycle was 20 miles (32.2 km) per hour.

  - William Ford gave his son a pocket watch when he turned 15. Henry immediately took it apart and then put it back together.

◀ Henry's first quadricycle was made with a metal frame. It was Henry's first working automobile, and he continued to improve the design.

Key Events

Henry formed the Ford Motor Company with new partners in 1903. The first Model T was produced in 1908. Customers bought more than 10,000 Model Ts that year. Ford's car cost only $850, while other companies charged thousands of dollars for their cars.

In 1913, Henry made changes to the way work was done in his factories. He outlined the steps needed to build the Model T and gave each worker a specific task. The car was built as it moved from worker to worker. This **assembly line** was first used to produce Ford cars at the factory in Highland Park, Michigan.

▲ By using an assembly line to construct his cars, Henry Ford was able to produce cars more quickly and at a lower cost. Assembly lines are still used in car manufacturing today.

Thoughts from Henry

Henry Ford used his imagination and skills to change the automobile industry. Here are some of the things he has said about his life and business.

Henry talks about his achievements.

"The Ford car blazed the way for the motor industry... It did a great deal, I am sure, to promote the growth and progress of this country."

Henry writes about curiosity.

"There is an immense amount to be learned simply by tinkering with things."

Henry believed in the power of positive thinking.

"Whether you think you can, or think you can't—you're right."

Henry talks about the importance of learning.

"Anyone who stops learning is old, whether at twenty or eighty. Anyone who keeps learning stays young. The greatest thing in life is to keep your mind young."

Henry talks about why he raced his cars.

"The 999 did what it was intended to do. It advertised the fact that I could build a fast motor car."

Henry talks about teamwork.

"Coming together is a beginning; keeping together is progress; working together is success."

What Is an Entrepreneur?

An entrepreneur is a person who runs his or her own business. Entrepreneurs may have an invention or a new way of doing something. They may need partners or investors to provide money to help them develop the business. Henry Ford had many partners in the different companies he started.

An entrepreneur is independent and is good at solving problems. Entrepreneurs believe in their ideas, even when others do not. An entrepreneur will not settle for 'good enough.' He or she strives for excellence. Henry was a perfectionist, and his partners did not always agree with his decisions. Two of his car companies failed.

Entrepreneurs are not always focused on making money, but the amount of money a business makes is one way to measure how successful it is.

▶ Henry was good friends with fellow entrepreneurs Thomas Edison and Harvey Firestone, as well as nature writer John Burroughs. The four went on many trips together.

INVESTORS

Most entrepreneurs need investors to help start their business. An investor is a person who provides money for an entrepreneur to develop his or her idea. The investor is taking a risk, hoping that the business will succeed. He or she hopes the business will make a **profit** by making more money than was put into it. Then, the investor will receive part of that profit.

Entrepreneur 101

Andrew Carnegie (1835–1919)

Andrew Carnegie was born in Scotland and moved to the United States when he was 13. He immediately went to work in a factory. Andrew eventually started the Carnegie Steel Company. He used new technology in his factories that helped him produce steel more quickly and cheaply. Andrew owned everything he needed to produce steel, including raw materials, ships, and railroads. He became extremely wealthy and donated millions of dollars to libraries and schools around the world.

Mary Kay Ash (1913–2001)

Mary Kay Ash was born in Hot Wells, Texas. She worked for companies that sold household items and gifts. In 1963, Mary Kay used $5,000 to start her own skin care business. Mary Kay Inc. sold almost $1 million worth of products in its first two years of operation. Today, more than 2.5 million salespeople work for Mary Kay Inc.

Sam Walton (1918–1992)

Sam Walton was born in Oklahoma. He earned a degree from the University of Missouri and then went to work for the department store, J.C. Penney. Sam opened the first Walmart store in Arkansas in 1962 with his brother, James. They focused on selling products at affordable prices. Unlike other major store chains, Sam put his stores in small towns rather than cities. The chain grew quickly. By 1985, there were 800 Walmart stores in the United States.

Steve Jobs (1955–2011)

Steve Jobs grew up in Mountain View, California, in an area known as the Silicon Valley. His father taught him to take things apart and rebuild them. In 1976, Steve started Apple Computers with his friend, computer engineer Steve Wozniak. The pair wanted to develop personal computers that were easy to use. Today, Apple continues to create new products such as the iPod, iPad, and iPhone.

Influences

Mary Ford was an important influence in her son's life. She taught Henry to expect difficult and unpleasant jobs in his life. He would need courage and self-discipline to do his best at every task he was given. She said to Henry, "You may have pity on others, but you must not have pity on yourself." He was very saddened when she died. He was only 12 years old.

Henry admired Thomas Edison, an inventor who studied electricity and developed useful products, such as the long-lasting electric light bulb. When Henry described his idea for creating a better gas engine, Thomas became very excited. He encouraged Henry to develop his plan. The two eventually became good friends and business partners.

▲ Clara Ford would often accompany her husband on business trips when he visited manufacturing facilities around the world.

Henry's greatest supporter was his wife, Clara. They met in 1885 and were married in 1888. Throughout their marriage, Clara remained supportive of her husband's plans, even when others thought they were too risky. At times, Henry admitted that Clara believed more strongly in his ideas than he did.

THE FORD FAMILY

Henry and Clara had one son. Edsel Bryant Ford was born November 6, 1893. Edsel took over as president of the Ford Motor Company in 1919, but his father remained in control of much of the company business. Then, in 1943, Edsel died. Henry was not healthy and grew more frail as he got older. Eventually his grandson, Henry Ford II, took full control of the company.

▲ While Henry was interested in the engineering and manufacturing of automobiles, Edsel was interested in working on the style and design of the cars the company produced.

Overcoming Obstacles

More than 240 companies were making cars in the United States between 1904 and 1908. Many of those companies failed. Even Henry did not have instant success, but he used what he learned from his failure to improve his idea. When other car companies came out with three or four new models each year, Henry focused on perfecting the design and production for the Model T.

Then, in 1929, the **Great Depression** changed everything. The **stock market** crashed in the United States, and investors all over the country lost their money. The strength of the Ford Motor Company weakened. Ford had major competition from two other car manufacturers, General Motors and Chrysler. Henry realized he needed something new and exciting to bring customers back. In 1932, he developed an eight-cylinder engine, known as the 'flathead.' The cylinders were arranged in V formation, creating a powerful engine. This new affordable V-8 engine was very popular and helped renew people's interest in Ford cars.

◀ From 1913 to 1925, the Model T was available only in black. Henry could cut time and costs by painting the car one color.

▲ In 1941, workers at the Ford manufacturing plant in River Rouge, Michigan, stopped work in protest after several union employees were let go.

During the Depression, the economy continued to decline. Henry was forced to cut pay and **lay off** thousands of workers. Workers were joining **unions** to try to get fair pay and better working conditions. Henry fought to keep the unions out of his factories. Union leaders often criticized Henry because he was a powerful leader in U.S. business. Protests at his River Rouge factory grew violent. Eventually, Henry signed an agreement with the United Automobile Workers union in 1941, putting an end to the strikes at his factories.

Achievements and Successes

Henry Ford dreamed of creating 'the **universal** car.' He wanted to build a car that everyone could afford, that was easy to operate, and easy to fix. The Model T was the answer to his dream. He developed a **franchise** system that allowed local companies to sell and fix Ford vehicles. In order to serve the growing number of automobiles on the road, more gas stations were popping up across the country.

The assembly line system that Henry created in 1913 was an even bigger success. Cars that once took several hours to build, now took only 93 minutes using the assembly line. In 1916, Henry was able to cut manufacturing costs and sold the Model T for $360. By 1918, almost half of all the cars on U.S. roads were Model Ts. Henry's factories provided jobs for thousands of workers. He shocked other business owners when he announced he would double the average worker's pay rate, raising it to $5 per day. He also shortened the work day to eight hours.

◀ Conveyor belts were added to the Ford factories in 1913. Conveyor belts moved the cars along a belt to each worker so that workers did not have to move to each car.

Henry's wealth grew, and he expanded into other businesses. He manufactured airplanes and boats, and owned a radio station, a coal mine, and a rubber plantation in Brazil. In 1940, Henry agreed to build airplane engines for the government. Soon, he was also making bombers, trucks, jeeps, tanks, and glider planes. When Henry Ford died in 1947, people remembered him as a hero of the modern world.

HELPING OTHERS

Education was important to Henry. Through his charity work, he helped people improve their own lives by teaching them important skills, rather than just giving them handouts. In 1911, he invited 10 homeless boys to live on his farm. They did chores on the farm and went to school. In 1916, Henry started the Henry Ford Trade School. The school taught trade skills, including auto mechanics, as well as traditional subjects such as mathematics. Henry, Clara, and Edsel Ford formed the Ford Foundation in 1936. The foundation was set up to help organizations in need. Today, the foundation continues to give millions of dollars to charitable projects.

▶ **The Ford Foundation provides money to projects that aim to reduce poverty and injustice, advance human achievement, and strengthen democratic values.**

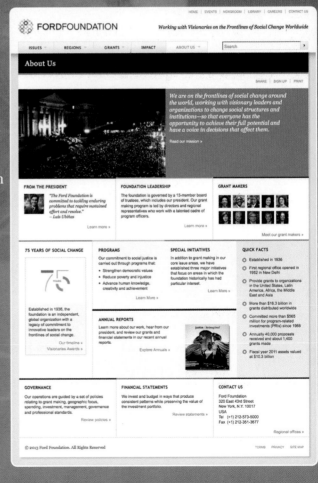

Write a Biography

A person's life story can be the subject of a book. This kind of book is called a biography. Biographies describe the lives of remarkable people, such as those who have achieved great success or have done important things to help others. These people may be alive today, or they may have lived many years ago. Reading a biography can help you learn more about a remarkable person.

At school, you might be asked to write a biography. First, decide who you want to write about. You can choose an entrepreneur, such as Henry Ford, or any other person. Then, find out if your library has any books about this person. Learn as much as you can about him or her. Write down the key events in this person's life. What was this person's childhood like? What has he or she accomplished? What are his or her goals? What makes this person special or unusual?

A concept web is a useful research tool. Read the questions in the following concept web. Answer the questions in your notebook. Your answers will help you write a biography.

Writing a Biography

Your Opinion
- What did you learn from the books you read in your research?
- Would you suggest these books to others?
- Was anything missing from these books?

Childhood
- Where and when was this person born?
- Describe his or her parents, siblings, and friends.
- Did this person grow up in unusual circumstances?

Adulthood
- Where does this individual currently reside?
- Does he or she have a family?

Main Accomplishments
- What is this person's life's work?
- Has he or she received awards or recognition for accomplishments?
- How have this person's accomplishments served others?

Work and Preparation
- What was this person's education?
- What was his or her work experience?
- How does this person work; what is or was the process he or she uses or used?

Help and Obstacles
- Did this individual have a positive attitude?
- Did he or she receive help from others?
- Did this person have a mentor?
- Did this person face any hardships?
- If so, how were the hardships overcome?

Timeline

YEAR	HENRY FORD	WORLD EVENTS
1863	Henry Ford is born on July 30.	James Plimpton invents the four-wheeled roller skate.
1903	Henry starts the Ford Motor Company.	The Wright brothers complete their first successful flight near Kitty Hawk, North Carolina.
1908	Ford Motor Company begins manufacturing the Model T.	The New York to Paris Auto Race is won in 169 days.
1913	The first automobile assembly line is introduced at Ford's Highland Park factory.	A Russian man, Igor Sikorsky, flies the first four-engine aircraft.
1932	Henry produces the V-8 engine.	The U.S. government begins to tax gasoline at one cent per gallon.
1941	Henry signs an agreement with the United Automobile Workers union.	Japan attacks Pearl Harbor, and the United States declares war on Japan.
1947	Henry Ford dies at age 83.	John Cobb sets a world land speed record, driving his motor vehicle at 394.2 miles (634.4 km) per hour.

Key Words

assembly line: a way of making a product, usually in a line formation. Each person or machine in the line does a specific task.

cylinder: a chamber in an engine that contains gas or liquid

franchise: a license given by a company to allow another person or company to sell its products

Great Depression: a time during the 1930s when there was economic difficulty because of a stock market crash. Many people lost their jobs and were unable to feed their families

lay off: when people lose their jobs, usually because a company does not have the money to pay them

manufacturing: making products with machines or manual labor

profit: the amount of money left after the costs of running a business have been paid

self-propelled: moving by itself, rather than being pulled or pushed

stock market: a place where shares in a company are traded

unions: organizations that represent workers

universal: something that is present everywhere

Index

Log on to www.av2books.com

AV² by Weigl brings you media enhanced books that support active learning. Go to www.av2books.com, and enter the special code found on page 2 of this book. You will gain access to enriched and enhanced content that supplements and complements this book. Content includes video, audio, weblinks, quizzes, a slide show, and activities.

AV² Online Navigation

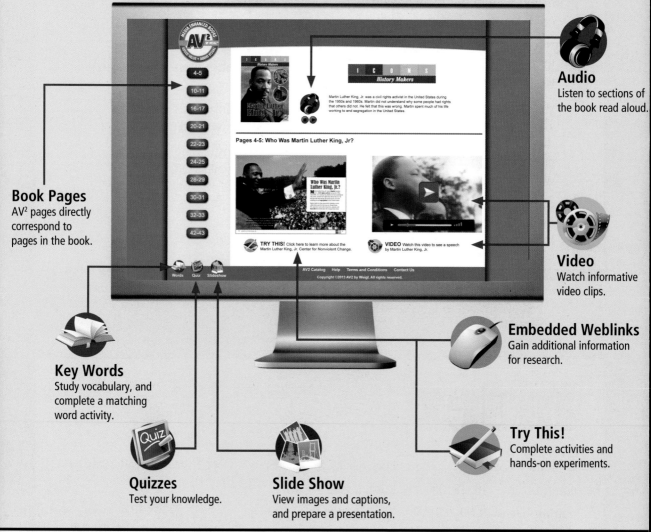

Audio
Listen to sections of the book read aloud.

Book Pages
AV² pages directly correspond to pages in the book.

Video
Watch informative video clips.

Key Words
Study vocabulary, and complete a matching word activity.

Embedded Weblinks
Gain additional information for research.

Try This!
Complete activities and hands-on experiments.

Quizzes
Test your knowledge.

Slide Show
View images and captions, and prepare a presentation.

AV² was built to bridge the gap between print and digital. We encourage you to tell us what you like and what you want to see in the future.

Sign up to be an AV² Ambassador at www.av2books.com/ambassador.